Classic

AMERICAN

Classic

AMERICAN

Home cooking from all over the USA

INTRODUCTION BY
ANNE MAGRUDER

SMITHMARK

This edition published in 1997 by
SMITHMARK Publishers, a division of US Media Holdings, Inc.
16 East 32nd Street
New York, New York 10016

SMITHMARK books are available for bulk purchase for sales promotion and for premium use. For details write or call
the manager of special sales, SMITHMARK Publishers, 16 East 32nd Street, New York, New York 10016; (212) 532-6600.

Produced by Anness Publishing Limited
Hermes House
88-89 Blackfriars Road
London SE1 8HA

ISBN 0 7651 9569 0

Publisher: Joanna Lorenz
Senior Food Editor: Linda Fraser
Project Editor: Zoe Antoniou
Designer: Ian Sandom
Illustrator: Madeleine David
Photographers: Karl Adamson, Edward Allwright, Steve Baxter,
Amanda Heywood and Michael Michaels
Recipes: Carla Capalbo, Frances Cleary, Roz Denny, Christine France, Sara Gates,
Shirley Gill, Patricia Lousada, Norma MacMillan, Laura Washburn and Steve Wheeler
Food for photography: Elizabeth Wolf-Cohen, Wendy Lee and Jane Stevenson
Stylists: Hilary Guy, Blake Minton and Kirsty Rawlings
Jacket photographer: Thomas Odulate

Printed and bound in Singapore

Picture on frontispiece shows a selection of food typical of the American
Midwest, including Country Meat Loaf and Butternut Squash Bisque.

1 3 5 7 9 10 8 6 4 2

CONTENTS

INTRODUCTION

What is classic American cooking? The quintessential American food – the hamburger – is a native of Germany. Chili con Carne, though it sounds spicy and foreign, is in fact considered a culinary travesty south of the Texas border. Pizza, quiche, pasta, fajitas and guacamole, while unquestionably foreign, are right at home on most "American" restaurant menus.

The stereotypical American is a rugged pioneer shaped by and shaping the endless frontier. But what he wants to eat is much closer to home: mother's cooking. The early settlers, for example, were no exception. Although the Pilgrims were grateful for the Indians' gift of corn, which kept them from starving during their first winter in North America, they planted wheat as soon as possible in order to duplicate the English breads and puddings they craved. They also imported beef, pork and all kinds of comfort foods from England to keep the home fires burning. Plenty of indigenous foods – among them corn, beans, clams, peanuts, cranberries and pumpkins – worked their way into the American repertoire, but the tone was and remains simple and homespun.

America is a nation made up of immigrants, all longing for the cooking they grew up eating, and in large cities, especially on the coasts, almost any ethnic food is available, from Polish to Peruvian. But if this country is a melting pot of cultures, its immigrant foods remain doggedly faithful to their homey origins. Within a few years of settling here, each immigrant group has made sure the ingredients they love are available. In the community gardens and backyards of our cities, an Italian-American fusses over fennel and tomatoes while his Vietnamese neighbor raises fresh cilantro and mint. Farmers' markets and supermarkets also abound with the traditional foods of all cultures.

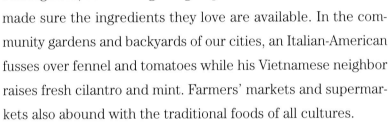

Those traditional foods have taken root, making America their home. Many Italian dishes – macaroni and cheese, spaghetti with tomato sauce – are now American classics. It is highly likely that in a century or so, after Vietnamese immigrants have settled more regions of the country, opening restaurants along the way, the aromatic noodle soup *pho* will show up in an all American cookbook. After all, the classic American dish, gumbo – a highly seasoned seafood stew – was originally African.

Picture on right shows a selection of muffins, rolls and tea breads, including cornbread, in the center.

A selection of Southwestern dishes, including chili con carne, cheese, soured cream, guacamole and nacho chips.

There are also many regional differences in eating habits that play a large part in defining American food. Seafood has always been popular in the coastal regions, for example, where oysters, clams and lobsters are plentiful. This has helped to shape the culinary heritage of New England as well as California. A wide range of seafood is now available in most supermarkets.

In the Southwest, a unique style of cooking has developed over the years which draws on Native American influences as well as the Mexican culture south of the border. These "Tex Mex" dishes, such as fajitas, are dominated by ingredients such as corn, tomatoes, beans, and are flavored of course by the hot chili pepper. They are popular everywhere and are enjoyed in many different restaurants.

In the Southern states, the mix of culinary influences is particularly diverse. History, over the years, has created many differing influences in the area, brought by French and Spanish settlers and African customs that were introduced through the slave trade. Combined again with Native American customs, this region has become home to many rich and tantalizing dishes; Cajun food is perhaps the most well-known. Southern Fried Chicken has become particularly popular elsewhere.

The Northwest and mountain states offer good hunting and fishing territory, which is also central to the American style of

Picture above shows a typical Thanksgiving scene.

cooking. There are many hearty meat dishes, such as meatloaf, that are very popular. The vast farmlands of the Midwest, however, emphasize the importance of baking, with their great fields of wheat and corn. Indeed, breads and cakes are now a way of life: delicious foods such as muffins, pies and cheesecake have become representative, to a certain extent, of the national cuisine. Home-grown ingredients remain very much at the heart of American cooking, as shown by the popularity of the vast number of local farmers' markets, prominent in cities and towns everywhere. Supermarkets also stock an enormous range of the ethnic foods that have become so much a part of America.

Basically, classic American cooking is whatever is cooking in American homes. The recipes in this book – with a few high-toned exceptions such as Oysters Rockefeller and Caesar Salad – are what is being served at barbecues, brunches and Sunday suppers all across the country. At first glance, it is a collection of exotic specialities – why else would Pork Fajitas exist alongside Quiche? Close up, you will see a trove of nostalgic foods that, though technically imported, are far from exotic. As bold, brash and pioneering as Americans may be, American cooks look homeward, deliciously, for comfort. It is such food that has become what is as American as Apple Pie itself.

BEEF CHILI SOUP

A hearty dish based on a traditional chili recipe. It is ideal with fresh crusty bread as a warming start to any meal.

INGREDIENTS
1 tablespoon oil
1 onion, chopped
6 ounces ground beef
2 garlic cloves, chopped
1 fresh red chili, sliced
2 tablespoons flour
1 can (14 ounces) chopped tomatoes
2¹/₂ cups beef stock
2 cups canned kidney beans, drained
2 tablespoons chopped fresh parsley, plus extra to garnish
salt and ground black pepper
crusty bread, to serve

SERVES 4

COOK'S TIP
For a milder flavor, remove the seeds from the chili before slicing.

1 Heat the oil in a large saucepan. Fry the onion and ground beef for 5 minutes until they begin to brown.

2 Add the garlic, chili and flour. Cook for 1 minute, then add the tomatoes and pour in the stock. Bring to a boil.

3 Stir in the kidney beans and season well. Cook for 20 minutes.

4 Add the parsley and season to taste. Pour into individual soup bowls, sprinkle with chopped parsley and serve immediately with fresh crusty bread.

FRESH TOMATO SOUP

T his brightly colored soup tastes best when made with meaty, flavorful Italian plum tomatoes. Serve it with plenty of fresh bread for a satisfying lunch, or sprinkle some croutons on top for a dinner party appetizer.

INGREDIENTS

2 tablespoons butter or margarine
1 onion, chopped
2 pounds sun-ripened tomatoes, quartered
2 carrots, chopped
2 cups chicken stock
2 tablespoons chopped fresh parsley
1/2 teaspoon fresh thyme leaves or
1/4 teaspoon dried thyme
1/3 cup whipping cream (optional)
salt and ground black pepper

SERVES 4

1 Melt the butter in a large saucepan. Add the onion and cook for about 5 minutes or until softened.

2 Stir in the tomatoes, carrots, chicken stock, parsley and thyme. Bring to a boil. Reduce the heat to low, cover the pan and simmer for 15–20 minutes until the carrots are tender.

3 Purée the soup in a vegetable mill. (Alternatively, use a blender or food processor, then strain to remove seeds.) Return the puréed soup to the saucepan.

4 Stir in the cream, if using, and reheat gently. Season with salt and pepper. Ladle into warmed soup bowls and serve hot, sprinkled with a little more thyme, if you wish.

BUTTERNUT SQUASH BISQUE

I f butternut squash is not available, make this dish with another variety of squash, such as pumpkin.

INGREDIENTS
2 tablespoons butter
or margarine
2 small onions, finely chopped
1 pound butternut squash, peeled,
seeded and diced
5 cups chicken stock
1 large baking potato, diced
1 teaspoon paprika
1/2 cup whipping
cream (optional)
1 1/2 teaspoon chopped fresh chives, plus
whole chives, to garnish
salt and ground black pepper

SERVES 4

1 Melt the butter in a large saucepan. Add the onions and cook for about 5 minutes, until softened.

2 Add the butternut squash, chicken stock, potatoes and paprika. Bring to a boil. Reduce the heat to low, cover the pan and simmer for about 35 minutes, until the vegetables are soft.

3 Pour the soup into a food processor or blender and process until smooth. Return the soup to the pan and stir in the cream, if using. Season with salt and pepper and reheat gently.

4 Stir in the chopped chives just before serving. If desired, garnish each serving with a few whole chives.

NEW ENGLAND CLAM CHOWDER

This tasty soup made from fresh clams is a real favorite in New England – try it out and see if it becomes one of your favorites!

INGREDIENTS
48 small clams, scrubbed
6 cups water
¼ cup finely diced salt pork
or bacon
1 onion, finely chopped
1 bay leaf
5 potatoes, diced
2 cups milk, warmed
1 cup light cream
chopped fresh parsley, to garnish
salt and ground black pepper

SERVES 8

1 Rinse the clams well in cold water and drain. Place them in a deep saucepan with the water and bring to a boil. Cover and steam for about 10 minutes until the shells open. Remove from the heat.

2 When the clams have cooled slightly, remove them from their shells, discarding any that have not opened. Chop them roughly, then strain the cooking liquid through a strainer lined with cheesecloth and reserve it.

3 In a large saucepan, fry the salt pork or bacon until it begins to brown. Add the onion and cook over low heat for 8–10 minutes, until softened.

4 Add the bay leaf, potatoes and clam cooking liquid. Stir, bring to a boil and simmer for 5–10 minutes.

5 Stir in the chopped clams and continue to cook until the potatoes are tender, stirring occasionally. Season with salt and pepper to taste.

6 Reduce the heat to low and stir in the warmed milk and the cream. Simmer very gently for 5 more minutes. Discard the bay leaf, taste and adjust the seasoning. Serve sprinkled with parsley.

COOK'S TIP
If the clams have been freshly dug, purging helps to rid them of all sand and stomach contents. Put them in a bowl of cold water, sprinkle with ½ cup cornmeal and some salt. Stir lightly and let stand in a cool place for 3–4 hours.

OYSTERS ROCKEFELLER

D on't be worried about preparing oysters – to open them up, just push the point of a strong-bladed knife a short way into the "hinge." Push down firmly. The lid should pop open.

INGREDIENTS
1 pound fresh spinach leaves
3 scallions, chopped
1 celery stalk, chopped
1/2 cup chopped fresh parsley
1 garlic clove
2 anchovy fillets
2 tablespoons butter or margarine
1/2 cup dry bread crumbs
1 teaspoon Worcestershire sauce
1 tablespoon anise-flavored liqueur
(Pernod or Ricard)
1/2 teaspoon salt
Tabasco sauce, to taste
36 oysters in their shells
thin strips of lemon rind, to garnish

SERVES 6

1 Wash the spinach well. Drain and place it in a heavy saucepan. Cover and cook over low heat until just wilted. Remove from the heat and, when cool enough to handle, squeeze to remove excess water.

2 Put the spinach, scallions, celery, parsley, garlic and anchovy fillets in a food processor or blender and chop finely.

3 Heat the butter in a small saucepan. Add the spinach mixture, dry bread crumbs, Worcestershire sauce, liqueur, salt and Tabasco sauce to taste. Cook for 1–2 minutes, then cool and chill until ready to use.

4 Preheat the oven to 450°F. Line a baking sheet with crumpled foil.

5 Open the oysters and remove the top shells. Arrange the oysters side by side on the foil (it will keep them upright). Spoon the spinach mixture over the oysters, smoothing the tops with the back of the spoon.

6 Bake for about 20 minutes, until piping hot. Serve immediately, garnished with thin strips of lemon rind.

NEW ENGLAND CLAMBAKE WITH LOBSTER

An exotic combination of fresh seaweed and lobsters makes this a bake that will certainly impress your guests.

INGREDIENTS
fresh seaweed
salt
6 lobsters, 1 pound each
2 pounds white onions, peeled
2 pounds small red potatoes
36 small clams
6 ears corn, husks and silk removed
1 cup butter or margarine
3 tablespoons chopped fresh chives

SERVES 6

1 Put a layer of seaweed in the bottom of a large deep saucepan containing 1 inch of salted water. Put the lobsters on top and cover with more seaweed.

2 Add the onions and potatoes. Cover the pan and bring the water to a boil.

3 After 10 minutes, add the clams and the corn. Cover again and cook until the clams have opened, the lobster shells are red, and the potatoes are tender. This should take 15–20 minutes.

4 Meanwhile, melt the butter in a small saucepan and stir in the chopped chives.

5 Discard the seaweed. Serve the lobsters and clams with the vegetables, accompanied by the chive butter.

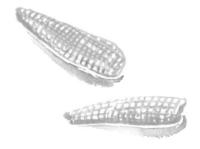

17

BAKED STUFFED CRAB

A wonderful looking dish that is surprisingly easy to make. Serve it as a dazzling main course for a dinner party with salad and rice.

INGREDIENTS
4 freshly cooked crabs
1 celery stalk, diced
1 scallion, finely chopped
1 small fresh green chili, seeded and
finely chopped
$1/3$ cup mayonnaise
2 tablespoons fresh lemon juice
1 tablespoon chopped fresh chives
$1/2$ cup fresh bread crumbs
$1/2$ cup Cheddar cheese, grated
2 tablespoons butter or
margarine, melted
salt and ground black pepper
fresh parsley sprigs, to garnish

SERVES 4

1 Preheat the oven to 375°F. Pull the claws and legs from each crab. Separate the body from the shell. Scoop out the meat from the shell. Discard the feathery gills and the intestines; remove the meat and coral from the body. Crack the claws and remove the meat.

2 Scrub the shells. Cut into the seam on the underside with scissors. The inner part of the shell should break off cleanly along the seam, enlarging the opening. Rinse the shells and dry them well.

3 In a bowl, combine the crabmeat, celery, scallion, chili, mayonnaise, lemon juice and chives. Season with salt and pepper to taste and mix well.

4 In another bowl, toss together the bread crumbs, cheese and melted butter.

5 Pile the crab mixture into the shells. Sprinkle with the bread crumb mixture and bake for about 20 minutes, until golden brown. Serve hot, garnished with sprigs of parsley.

CAJUN BLACKENED SWORDFISH

T his spicy fish dish will bring a ray of Cajun sunshine into your home at any time of the year.

INGREDIENTS
4 tablespoons butter or margarine
4 (6-ounce) swordfish steaks
2 teaspoons each paprika, dried thyme and oregano
1 teaspoon onion powder
1 teaspoon garlic salt
1 teaspoon ground cumin
1 teaspoon each mustard powder
1 teaspoon cayenne
1/2 teaspoon salt and 1 teaspoon pepper
boiled rice, to serve
dill sprigs, to garnish

SERVES 4

1 Melt the butter and brush both sides of the fish steaks with it.

2 Combine all the spices, herbs and seasonings and coat both sides of the fish steaks with it, rubbing it in well. Then heat a heavy frying pan for about 5 minutes or until a drop of water sprinkled on the surface sizzles.

3 Drizzle 2 teaspoons of the remaining butter over the fish steaks. Add the steaks to the frying pan, butter-side down, and cook for 2–3 minutes, or until the underside is blackened.

4 Drizzle another 2 teaspoons melted butter over the fish, then turn the steaks over. Cook for 2–3 minutes more, until the second side is blackened and the fish flakes easily when tested with a fork.

5 Serve the fish on a bed of rice, garnish with dill and drizzle the remaining butter on top.

SEAFOOD AND SAUSAGE GUMBO

When you serve this meal, make sure that each person gets both seafood and sausage on their plate.

INGREDIENTS
3 pounds whole raw shrimp
7¹/₂ cups water
1 onion, quartered
4 bay leaves
³/₄ cup oil
1 cup flour
4 tablespoons margarine or butter
3 large onions, finely chopped
1 green bell pepper, seeded and chopped
2 large celery stalks, chopped
1¹/₂ pounds kielbasa (Polish) or andouille
sausage, cut in ¹/₂-inch rounds
1 pound fresh okra, cut in
¹/₂-inch slices
3 garlic cloves, finely chopped
¹/₂ teaspoon fresh or dried thyme leaves
2 teaspoons salt
¹/₂ teaspoon ground black pepper
¹/₂ teaspoon ground white pepper
1 teaspoon cayenne pepper
Tabasco sauce (optional)
1 can (14 ounces) chopped tomatoes
1 pound fresh crabmeat
rice, to serve

SERVES 10–12

1 Peel and devein the shrimp; reserve the heads and shells. Keep the shrimp in a covered bowl in the fridge while you make the sauce.

2 Put the heads and shells in a saucepan with the water, quartered onion and 1 bay leaf. Bring to a boil, then partly cover and simmer for 20 minutes. Strain, reserving the stock, and set aside.

3 Heat the oil in a cast-iron or steel pan. (Do not use a non-stick pan.) When the oil is hot, add the flour, a little at a time, and mix to a smooth paste using a wooden spoon.

4 Cook over medium-low heat, stirring frequently, until the Cajun roux, the sauce base, reaches the desired color. It will take 25–40 minutes for the roux to deepen gradually in color from light beige to tan to a deeper, redder brown. When it reaches the color of peanut butter, remove the pan from the heat and continue stirring until the roux has cooled and stopped cooking.

5 Melt the margarine in a large heavy saucepan. Add the onions, green pepper and celery. Cook over medium-low heat for 6–8 minutes, stirring occasionally, until the onions are softened.

6 Add the sausage and cook for 5 minutes. Stir in the okra and garlic, and cook until the okra stops producing white "threads."

7 Add the other bay leaves, thyme, salt, black and white pepper, cayenne and Tabasco sauce to taste, if desired. Mix well. Stir in 6 cups of the shrimp stock and the tomatoes. Bring to a boil, then partly cover the pan, lower the heat and simmer for about 20 minutes.

8 Whisk in the Cajun roux. Raise the heat and bring the mixture to a boil, whisking well. Lower the heat again and simmer, uncovered, for 40–50 minutes more, stirring occasionally.

9 Gently stir in the shrimp and crabmeat. Cook for 3–4 minutes, until the shrimp turn pink. To serve, put a mound of hot rice in each serving bowl and ladle the gumbo on top.

SOUTHERN FRIED CHICKEN

Simply serve these spicy chicken pieces with fresh rolls or biscuits for a taste of the South.

INGREDIENTS
1/2 cup buttermilk
1 chicken (3 pounds), cut in pieces
oil, for frying
1/2 cup flour
1 tablespoon paprika
1/4 teaspoon pepper
1 tablespoon water

SERVES 4

1 Put the buttermilk in a bowl and add the chicken. Stir, and set aside for 5 minutes.

2 Heat a 1/4-inch layer of oil in a large frying pan over medium-high heat. Do not let the oil overheat.

3 In a bowl or plastic bag, combine the flour, paprika and pepper. One by one, lift the chicken pieces out of the buttermilk and dip into the flour to coat, shaking off any excess.

4 Add the chicken pieces to the hot oil and fry for about 10 minutes until lightly browned, turning over halfway through the cooking time.

5 Reduce the heat to low and add the water to the frying pan. Cover and cook for 30 minutes, turning the pieces over at 10-minute intervals. Uncover the pan and continue cooking for about 15 minutes, until the chicken is very tender and the coating is crisp, turning every 5 minutes. Serve hot.

SAN FRANCISCO CHICKEN WINGS

C hicken wings baked in a tangy sauce create a delicious meal. Serve with boiled potatoes and a crisp green salad.

INGREDIENTS
⅓ cup soy sauce
1 tablespoon light brown sugar
1 tablespoon rice vinegar
2 tablespoons dry sherry
juice of 1 orange
2-inch strip of orange peel
1 star anise
1 teaspoon cornstarch
¼ cup water
1 tablespoon chopped fresh ginger
*¼ teaspoon Asian chili-garlic sauce,
to taste*
*22–24 chicken wings,
tips removed*

SERVES 4

1 Preheat the oven to 400°F. Combine the soy sauce, brown sugar, vinegar, sherry, orange juice and peel and star anise in a saucepan. Bring to a boil over medium heat.

2 Combine the cornstarch and water in a small bowl and stir until blended. Add to the boiling soy sauce mixture, stirring well. Boil for 1 minute more, stirring constantly.

3 Remove the soy sauce mixture from the heat and stir in the chopped ginger and chili-garlic sauce.

4 Arrange the chicken wings in one layer in a large baking dish. Pour the soy sauce mixture on top and stir to coat the chicken wings evenly.

5 Bake for 30–40 minutes, basting occasionally, until tender and browned. Serve the wings hot or warm.

COUNTRY MEAT LOAF

A crispy bacon shell holds this meat loaf together. Slice it thickly to serve to your guests with a fresh green vegetable and mashed potatoes.

INGREDIENTS
2 tablespoons butter or margarine
1 small onion, finely chopped
2 garlic cloves, finely chopped
1 celery stalk, finely chopped
1 pound lean ground beef
8 ounces ground veal or lamb
8 ounces lean ground pork
2 eggs
1 cup fresh bread crumbs
1/2 cup chopped fresh parsley
2 tablespoons chopped fresh basil
1/2 teaspoon fresh or dried thyme leaves
1/2 teaspoon salt
1/2 teaspoon ground black pepper
2 tablespoons Worcestershire sauce
1/4 cup chili sauce
or ketchup
6 slices bacon
fresh parsley and basil leaves, to garnish

SERVES 6

1 Preheat the oven to 350°F. Melt the butter over low heat. Add the onion, garlic and celery and cook for 8–10 minutes until softened. Remove from the heat and cool slightly.

2 Combine the onion, garlic and celery with all the other ingredients except the bacon. Mix together lightly, using a fork or your fingers. Do not overmix or the meat loaf will be too tough.

3 Shape the meat mixture into an oval loaf. Transfer it to a shallow baking tin.

4 Drape the bacon slices across the meat loaf. Bake for 1¼ hours, basting it with the juices and bacon fat in the pan.

5 Remove the loaf from the oven and drain off the fat. Allow to stand for a few minutes before serving the loaf garnished with fresh parsley and basil leaves.

RED FLANNEL HASH

The potatoes absorb the beet color and flavor to make this a hash with a difference.

INGREDIENTS
6 slices bacon
2 small onions, finely chopped
6 potatoes, boiled and diced
4 ounces corned beef, chopped
9 ounces cooked beets, diced
¹/₄ cup light cream or half-and-half
1 tablespoon chopped fresh parsley
salt and ground black pepper
fresh parsley sprigs, to garnish

SERVES 4

1 Fry the bacon until golden and beginning to crisp. Remove and drain on paper towels. Pour off all but 2 tablespoons of the bacon fat in the pan, reserving the rest.

2 Cut the bacon into ½-inch pieces and transfer to a mixing bowl. Cook the onions in the bacon fat over low heat for 8–10 minutes until softened. Remove from the pan and add to the bacon. Mix in the potatoes, corned beef, beets, cream and parsley. Season with salt and pepper and mix well.

3 Heat 4 tablespoons of the reserved bacon fat, or other fat, in the frying pan. Add the hash mixture, spreading it evenly over the base with a spatula. Cook over low heat for about 15 minutes, until the base is brown. Flip the hash out onto a plate.

4 Slide the hash back into the pan and cook the other side until browned. Serve immediately garnished with fresh parsley.

PORK FAJITAS

ajitas make a wonderful meal and diners can assemble their own at the table, to ensure satisfaction.

INGREDIENTS
juice of 3 limes
6 tablespoons olive oil
1 teaspoon dried oregano
1 teaspoon ground cumin
1/2 teaspoon red pepper flakes
1 1/2 pounds pork tenderloin,
cut in 3 1/2-inch strips
2 large onions, halved and thinly sliced
1 large green bell pepper, seeded and
thinly sliced lengthwise
salt

TO SERVE
12–15 flour tortillas, warmed
tomato salsa, guacamole, sour cream,
lettuce and fresh parsley

SERVES 6

1 Combine the lime juice, 3 tablespoons of the oil, oregano, cumin and red pepper. Add the pork pieces and turn to coat. Cover and let sit for 1 hour or chill overnight.

2 Remove the pieces of pork from the marinade. Pat them dry and season well.

3 Heat a ridged grill pan. When hot, add the pork and cook over high heat for 10–12 minutes, turning occasionally, until browned on all sides and cooked through.

4 Meanwhile, heat the remaining oil in a large frying pan. Add the onions and green pepper. Stir in 1/2 teaspoon of salt, and cook for about 15 minutes, until the vegetables are very soft, stirring occasionally. Remove and set aside.

5 Slice the pork pieces into thin strips. Add to the onion mixture and reheat briefly if necessary.

6 Spoon a little of the pork mixture onto each tortilla. Spread on some salsa, guacamole and sour cream, and roll up. Serve with extra salsa and some crisp lettuce, and garnish with fresh parsley.

TURKEY BREASTS WITH TOMATO AND CORN SALSA

 spicy salsa combines with grilled turkey breasts for a true taste of the Midwest.

INGREDIENTS
4 skinless, boneless turkey
breast halves (6 ounces each)
2 tablespoons fresh lemon juice
2 tablespoons olive oil
$1/2$ teaspoon ground cumin
$1/2$ teaspoon dried oregano
1 teaspoon coarse black pepper
salt
lettuce leaves, to serve

FOR THE SALSA
1 fresh green chili pepper
1 pound tomatoes, seeded and chopped
$1^{1}/_{2}$ cups corn, freshly cooked or
thawed if frozen
3 scallions, chopped
1 tablespoon chopped fresh parsley
2 tablespoons chopped fresh cilantro
2 tablespoons fresh lemon juice
3 tablespoons olive oil
1 teaspoon salt

SERVES 4

1 With a meat mallet or rolling pin, pound the turkey breasts between two sheets of waxed paper until thin.

2 In a shallow dish, combine the lemon juice, olive oil, cumin, oregano and pepper. Add the turkey and turn to coat. Cover and let stand for at least 2 hours, or chill overnight.

3 For the salsa, roast the chili over a gas flame, holding it with tongs, until charred on all sides. (Alternatively, char the skin under the broiler.) Let cool for about 5 minutes. Wearing rubber gloves, carefully rub off the charred skin. For a milder flavor, discard the seeds. Chop the chili finely and place in a bowl.

4 Add the remaining salsa ingredients to the chili in the bowl and toss well to blend. Set aside.

5 Remove the turkey from the marinade. Season it lightly with salt to taste on both sides.

6 Heat a ridged grill pan. When it is hot, add the turkey breasts and cook for about 3 minutes, until browned. Turn the meat over and and grill it on the other side for 3–4 more minutes, until cooked through. Serve immediately, accompanied by the salsa and crisp lettuce leaves.

CHEESEBURGERS

Loved by all kids, homemade burgers are hard to beat. Served with fries in a lightly toasted bun, this burger is bound together with bulgur wheat, which is actually good for you!

INGREDIENTS

½ cup bulgur wheat
1 pound ground beef
1 onion
1 tablespoon chopped fresh parsley
1 tablespoon tomato paste
1 tablespoon grated Parmesan cheese
1 egg, lightly beaten
4 hamburger buns, lightly toasted
lettuce leaves
4 slices cheese
salt and ground black pepper
fries and ketchup, to serve
fresh parsley sprigs, to garnish

SERVES 4

1 Place the bulgur wheat in a bowl and add enough boiling water to cover. Let stand for 10 minutes. Drain off any excess liquid if you need to.

2 Put the ground beef into a bowl and break it up with a fork.

3 Place the onion and parsley in a food processor or blender and process for 20 seconds. Add to the beef.

4 Stir in the tomato paste and grated Parmesan cheese. Season well and add the drained bulgur wheat.

5 Mix in the beaten egg. Shape into four patties with your hands. Cook for 8–10 minutes on each side in a medium hot oven or until cooked through.

6 Split the hamburger buns in half and place a hamburger inside each one with some lettuce leaves. Top with a slice of cheese and the hamburger bun top. Serve with fries and ketchup, garnished with fresh parsley.

BARBECUED SPARERIBS

Remember to provide finger bowls for your guests when serving spareribs – they can be very messy to eat!

INGREDIENTS
3 pounds meaty pork spareribs
¹/₂ cup oil
¹/₂ teaspoon paprika
crusty bread, to serve

FOR THE SAUCE
¹/₂ cup light brown sugar, firmly packed
2 teaspoons mustard powder
1 teaspoon salt
¹/₈ teaspoon pepper
¹/₂ teaspoon ground ginger
¹/₂ cup tomato sauce
¹/₂ cup fresh orange juice
1 small onion, finely chopped
1 garlic clove, finely chopped
2 tablespoons chopped fresh parsley
1 tablespoon Worcestershire sauce

SERVES 4

1 Preheat the oven to 375°F. Arrange the ribs in one overlapping layer in a roasting pan.

2 In a small bowl, combine the oil and paprika. Brush the mixture over the spareribs. Bake for 55–60 minutes, until the ribs are slightly crisp.

3 Combine the sauce ingredients in a small pan and bring to a boil. Simmer for about 5 minutes, stirring occasionally.

4 Pour off the fat from the roasting pan. Brush the spareribs with half of the sauce and bake for 20 more minutes. Turn the ribs over, brush with the remaining sauce and bake for 20 minutes longer. Cut into sections and serve

CHILLI CON CARNE

A classic recipe that has become a regular feature in many homes. Simple and economical, it is one of the most popular of all ground beef recipes.

INGREDIENTS

1 tablespoon oil
2 cups ground beef
1 onion, quartered
1 teaspoon chili powder
2 tablespoons flour
2 tablespoons tomato paste
²/₃ cup beef stock
1 can (7 ounces) chopped tomatoes
1 can (7 ounces) kidney beans, drained
1 green bell pepper, seeded and chopped
1 tablespoon Worcestershire sauce
¹/₂ cup long grain rice
salt
sour cream, to serve
chopped fresh parsley, to garnish

SERVES 4

1 Heat the oil in a large pan and fry the ground beef, onion and chili powder for 7 minutes.

2 Add the flour and tomato paste and cook for 1 minute. Stir in the stock and tomatoes and bring to a boil.

3 Add the kidney beans, green pepper and Worcestershire sauce. Reduce the heat and simmer for 45 minutes.

4 Meanwhile, cook the rice in boiling salted water for 10–12 minutes. Drain well and spoon onto a serving plate. Spoon the chili over the rice, add a spoonful of sour cream and garnish with parsley.

STUFFED POTATO SKINS

Customize your potato skins by adding any of your favorite herbs or spices to the potato mixture. You can experiment to create your own variations on this dish.

INGREDIENTS
3 baking potatoes (12 ounces each),
scrubbed and patted dry
1 tablespoon oil
3 tablespoons butter
1 onion, chopped
1 green bell pepper, seeded and
roughly chopped
1 teaspoon paprika
1 cup Cheddar cheese,
roughly grated
salt and ground black pepper
crisp green lettuce, to serve
fresh parsley, to garnish

SERVES 6

1 Preheat the oven to 450°F. Brush the potatoes all over with the oil and prick them with a fork.

2 Place the potatoes in a baking dish. Bake for about 1½ hours, or until tender.

3 Meanwhile, heat the butter in a large non-stick frying pan. Add the onion and a little salt and cook over medium heat for about 5 minutes, until softened. Add the chopped green pepper and continue cooking for 2–3 minutes until it is just tender but still slightly crunchy. Stir in the paprika and set aside.

4 When the potatoes are cooked, halve them lengthwise. Scoop out the flesh, keeping the pieces rough. Keep the potato skins warm.

VARIATION
For Bacon-Stuffed Potato Skins, add ¼ cup chopped cooked bacon to the cooked potato flesh and vegetables. Stuff as above.

5 Preheat the broiler. Add the potato flesh to the frying pan and cook over high heat, stirring, until it is lightly browned. Season with black pepper.

6 Divide the vegetable mixture evenly among the potato skin shells.

7 Sprinkle the grated cheese over the top. Broil the potatoes for 3–5 minutes, until the cheese just melts. Serve them immediately with a crisp green salad and garnish with fresh parsley.

CREAMY COLESLAW

Coleslaw is a great accompaniment to any main dish. Serve this one with Southern Fried Chicken and fries for a great lunch.

INGREDIENTS
1 head white cabbage, cut in wedges and cored
1/3 head red cabbage, cored
3 scallions, finely chopped
2 carrots, roughly grated
1 teaspoon sugar
2 tablespoons fresh lemon juice
2 teaspoons white wine vinegar
1/2 cup sour cream
1/2 cup mayonnaise
3/4 teaspoon celery seeds
salt and ground black pepper

SERVES 6

1 Slice the white and red cabbage very thinly across the leaves.

2 Place the cabbage in a mixing bowl and add the scallions and grated carrot. Toss to combine.

3 In a small bowl, combine the sugar, lemon juice, vinegar, sour cream, mayonnaise and celery seeds.

4 Pour the mayonnaise dressing over the vegetables. Season with salt and pepper. Stir until well coated and spoon into a serving bowl.

POTATO SALAD

or a change, you could use small red potatoes to give an attractive color to this salad.

INGREDIENTS

3 pounds small new potatoes
2 tablespoons white wine vinegar
1 tablespoon Dijon mustard
3 tablespoons olive oil
1 red onion, finely chopped
1/2 cup mayonnaise
2 tablespoons chopped fresh tarragon or
1 1/2 teaspoon dried tarragon
1/2 celery stalk, thinly sliced
salt and ground black pepper

SERVES 8

1 Cook the unpeeled potatoes in boiling salted water for 15–20 minutes, until just tender. Drain thoroughly.

2 In a small bowl, combine the vinegar and mustard until the mustard dissolves. Whisk in the oil.

3 When the potatoes are cool enough to handle, use a sharp knife to slice them into a large mixing bowl.

4 Add the onion to the potatoes and pour the dressing over them. Season, then toss gently to combine. Let stand for at least 30 minutes.

5 Combine the mayonnaise and tarragon. Stir gently into the potatoes along with the celery. Taste, and adjust the seasoning before serving.

ASPARAGUS, CORN AND RED BELL PEPPER QUICHE

he delicate flavors of asparagus and corn make this a heavenly quiche for all to enjoy.

INGREDIENTS

1²/₃ cups flour

¹/₂ teaspoon salt

³/₄ cup vegetable shortening

2–3 tablespoons very cold water

8 ounces fresh asparagus, woody stalks removed

2 tablespoons butter or margarine

1 small onion, finely chopped

1 red bell pepper, seeded and chopped

¹/₂ cup drained canned or frozen corn, thawed

2 eggs

1 cup light cream or half-and-half

¹/₂ cup Cheddar cheese, roughly grated

salt and ground black pepper

SERVES 6

1 Preheat the oven to 400°F. Sift the flour and salt into a bowl. Rub in the shortening until the mixture resembles coarse bread crumbs. Sprinkle in the cold water, 1 tablespoon at a time, tossing the mixture lightly with your fingertips or a fork until the dough forms a ball.

2 Roll out the pastry and use it to line a 10-inch quiche dish or loose-bottomed tart tin. Trim off excess pastry.

3 Line the pastry case with parchment paper and weigh it down with dry beans. Bake for 10 minutes. Remove the paper and beans and bake for about 5 more minutes, until the pastry case is set and beige in color. Leave to cool.

4 Trim the stem ends of eight of the asparagus spears to make them 4 inches long. Set aside.

5 Finely chop the asparagus trimmings and any remaining spears. Place in the bottom of the pastry case.

6 Melt the butter in a frying pan. Add the onion and red bell pepper and cook for about 5 minutes, until the vegetables are softened. Stir in the corn and cook for 2 more minutes.

7 Spoon the corn mixture over the chopped asparagus in the pastry case. In a small bowl, beat the eggs with the cream. Stir in the cheese and salt and pepper to taste. Pour into the pastry case.

8 Arrange the reserved asparagus spears like spokes of a wheel on top of the filling. Bake for 25–30 minutes, until the filling is set.

CAESAR SALAD

 classic salad combining hard-cooked eggs with lettuce in a tangy dressing, topped with garlic croutons.

INGREDIENTS
2 eggs
1 garlic clove, finely chopped
$^{1}/_{2}$ teaspoon salt
$^{1}/_{2}$ cup olive oil
juice of 1 lemon
$^{1}/_{4}$ teaspoon Worcestershire sauce
1 head Romaine lettuce, torn into
bite-size pieces
$^{1}/_{2}$ cup grated Parmesan cheese
ground black pepper
8 canned anchovy fillets, drained and
blotted dry on paper towels (optional)

FOR THE CROUTONS
1 garlic clove
$^{1}/_{4}$ teaspoon salt
$^{1}/_{4}$ cup olive oil
4 slices French bread, cubed

SERVES 4

1 Preheat the oven to 350°F. For the croutons, crush the garlic with the salt in a mixing bowl and stir in the oil. Add the bread cubes to the bowl and toss to coat with the garlic oil.

2 Spread the bread cubes on a baking sheet. Bake for 20–25 minutes, until golden brown.

3 Meanwhile, put the eggs in a small pan of boiling water and simmer gently for 7 minutes. Transfer to a bowl of cold water and shell them as soon as they are cool enough to handle.

4 Mash the garlic clove with the salt in the bottom of a salad bowl. Then, carefully whisk in the olive oil, lemon juice and Worcestershire sauce.

5 Add the lettuce to the salad bowl and toss well to coat with the dressing. Add the grated Parmesan cheese and season well with pepper. Add the croutons and toss to combine.

6 Cut the hard-cooked eggs into quarters. Arrange on top of the salad with the anchovies, if using. Serve immediately.

GUACAMOLE

This versatile dip can be served as an accompaniment to many dishes. Try it with fajitas, tortilla chips or a selection of mixed raw vegetables.

INGREDIENTS
3 large ripe avocados
3 scallions, finely chopped
1 garlic clove, finely chopped
1 tablespoon olive oil
1 tablespoon sour cream
1/2 teaspoon salt
2 tablespoons fresh lemon juice
sliced mixed bell peppers, to serve

MAKES 2 CUPS

1 Halve the avocados and remove the pits. Peel the halves. Put the avocado flesh in a large bowl.

2 Using a fork, mash all the avocado flesh coarsely.

3 Add the scallions, garlic, olive oil, sour cream, salt and lemon juice. Mash until well blended, but do not overmix the mixture. Small chunks of avocado should still remain. Taste the guacamole and adjust the seasoning, if necessary, with more salt or lemon juice.

4 Transfer to a serving bowl. Serve with slices of pepper for dipping.

COOK'S TIP
Guacamole does not keep well but, if necessary, it can be stored in the fridge for a few hours. Cover the surface with plastic wrap to prevent it from discoloring.

BOSTON BAKED BEANS

A bubbling casserole of white beans and salt pork provides a nutritious and satisfying meal for the whole family to enjoy.

INGREDIENTS

3 cups dried white beans, soaked
overnight
1 bay leaf
4 cloves
2 onions
½ cup molasses
¾ cup dark brown sugar
1 tablespoon Dijon mustard
1 teaspoon salt
1 teaspoon pepper
1 cup boiling water
8-ounce piece salt pork

SERVES 8

1 Drain and rinse the beans. Put them in a large saucepan with the bay leaf and cover with cold water. Bring to a boil and simmer for 1½–2 hours, until tender. Drain.

2 Preheat the oven to 275°F. Put the beans in a large ovenproof dish. Stick two cloves into each of the onions and add them to the dish.

3 In a mixing bowl, combine the molasses, sugar, mustard, salt and pepper. Add the boiling water and stir to mix.

4 Pour this mixture over the beans. Add more water, if necessary, so that the beans are almost covered with liquid.

5 Blanch the piece of salt pork in boiling water for 3 minutes. Drain. Score the rind in deep cuts ½ inch apart. Add the salt pork to the dish and push it down just below the surface of the beans, skin-side up.

6 Cover the dish and bake in the center of the oven for 4½–5 hours. Uncover for the last 30 minutes, so that the pork rind becomes brown and crisp. Slice or shred the pork and serve hot.

BAKED ACORN SQUASH WITH HERBS

I f you can't get hold of acorn squash, make this dish with a variety of winter squash available at your local greengrocer – the result will be just as good.

INGREDIENTS
2 acorn squash
6 tablespoons chopped fresh chives,
thyme, basil and parsley
4 tablespoons butter or margarine
salt and ground black pepper
mixed fresh herbs, to garnish

SERVES 4

1 Cut each squash in half crosswise and scoop out the seeds and stringy fibers. If necessary, cut a small slice off the base of each squash half so it sits level.

2 Preheat the oven to 375°F. Divide the chopped herbs into four parts and spoon into the hollows in the squash halves.

3 Top each half with butter and season with salt and pepper.

4 Arrange the squash halves in a shallow baking dish large enough to hold them in one layer. Pour boiling water into the bottom of the dish to a depth of about 1 inch. Cover the squash loosely with a piece of foil.

5 Bake for 45 minutes to 1 hour, until the squash is tender when tested with a fork. Serve hot, keeping the halves upright, garnished with fresh herbs.

MACARONI AND CHEESE

he crusty cheese topping makes this Macaroni and Cheese just that much more special.

INGREDIENTS
1 cup elbow macaroni
4 tablespoons butter or margarine
¹/₄ cup flour
2¹/₂ cups milk
1¹/₂ cups Cheddar cheese, grated
2 tablespoons finely chopped fresh parsley
1 cup dry breadcrumbs
¹/₂ cup grated Parmesan cheese
salt and ground black pepper

SERVES 4

1 Preheat the oven to 350°F. Grease a 10-inch gratin dish, then cook the macaroni in a large pan of boiling salted water until just tender to the bite (check the directions on the package for exact timing). Drain the pasta well.

2 Melt the butter in a pan. Add the flour and cook for 2 minutes, stirring, then stir in the milk. Bring to a boil, stirring constantly, and simmer for about 5 minutes, until thickened.

3 Remove the pan from the heat. Add the cooked macaroni, Cheddar cheese and parsley to the sauce and mix well. Season with salt and pepper.

4 Transfer the mixture to the prepared gratin dish, spreading it out evenly with a spoon.

5 Mix the bread crumbs and Parmesan cheese together with a fork and sprinkle over the macaroni.

6 Bake for 30–35 minutes, until the top is golden brown and the macaroni mixture is bubbling.

EGGS BENEDICT

f possible, use free-range eggs for this dish, as they have a vibrant yellow color.

INGREDIENTS

3 egg yolks
2 tablespoons fresh lemon juice
¼ teaspoon salt
8 tablespoons butter
2 tablespoons light cream or half-and-half
1 teaspoon vinegar
4 fresh eggs
2 English muffins or 4 slices of bread
butter, for spreading
2 thick slices of cooked ham
white pepper
fresh chives, to garnish
lettuce and tomato salad, to serve

SERVES 4

1 Blend the yolks, lemon juice and salt in a food processor or blender for 15 seconds.

2 Melt the butter until it bubbles (do not let it brown). With the motor running, pour the hot butter into the food processor or blender in a slow, steady stream. Turn off the machine as soon as all the butter has been added.

3 Transfer the sauce to the top of a double boiler or into a bowl set over a pan of just-simmering water. Stir for 2–3 minutes, until thickened. (If the sauce curdles, whisk in 1 tablespoon of boiling water.) Stir in the cream and season with white pepper. Keep warm over the hot water.

4 Bring a shallow saucepan of water to a boil. Stir in the vinegar. Break two of the eggs into separate cups, then slide them carefully into the gently simmering water. Delicately turn the white around the yolk with a slotted spoon. Cook until the eggs are set to your taste, for 3–4 minutes. Place them on paper towels to drain. Repeat with the remaining eggs. Very gently cut any ragged edges off the eggs with a small knife or scissors.

5 While the eggs are poaching, split and toast the muffins or toast the bread slices. Butter while still warm.

6 Cut the ham slices in half crosswise and brown them in butter, if desired. Place them on each muffin half or slice of toast. Trim the ham to fit neatly. Place an egg on each ham-topped muffin. Spoon the warm sauce over the eggs, garnish with chives and serve with a lettuce and tomato salad.

CORNBREAD

Squares of golden bread served with butter, or just on their own, are bound to be a hit with anyone feeling hungry around the house.

INGREDIENTS
2 eggs, lightly beaten
1 cup buttermilk
1 cup flour
1 cup cornmeal
2 teaspoons baking powder
¹/₂ teaspoon salt
1 tablespoon sugar
1 cup Cheddar cheese, grated
1 cup corn kernels, cut from
2 ears of fresh corn or thawed
if frozen

MAKES 9

1 Preheat the oven to 400°F. Grease a 9-inch square baking pan.

2 Put the eggs and buttermilk in a small mixing bowl and whisk until well combined. Set aside.

3 In another bowl, combine the flour, cornmeal, baking powder, salt and sugar. Pour in the egg mixture and stir with a wooden spoon until just combined. Mix in the cheese and corn.

4 Pour the batter into the prepared pan. Bake for about 25 minutes, until a skewer inserted in the center comes out clean.

5 Unmold the cornbread onto a wire rack and let cool completely. Cut into 3-inch squares for serving.

PIZZA

dapt this recipe to suit your tastes: let your imagination run wild with toppings of your choice!

INGREDIENTS
5 cups flour
1 teaspoon salt
2 teaspoons yeast
1¹/₄ cups lukewarm water
¹/₄ cup olive oil

FOR THE TOPPING
tomato sauce
grated Cheddar cheese
olives and herbs

MAKES 2

1 Mix the flour and salt and make a well in the center. Add the yeast, water and 2 tablespoons of olive oil. Let sit for 15 minutes.

2 Stir the dough until it just holds together. Knead until smooth and elastic. Avoid adding too much flour while kneading.

3 Brush the inside of a bowl with oil. Place the dough in the bowl and roll around to coat with the oil. Cover with a plastic bag and let rise in a warm place for about 45 minutes, until doubled in volume.

4 Divide the dough into two balls. Preheat the oven to 400°F.

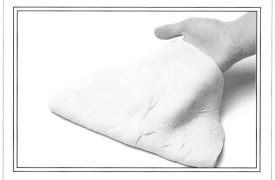

5 Roll each ball into a 10-inch circle. Flip the circles over and onto your palm. Set each circle on the work surface and rotate, stretching the dough as you turn, until they are about 12 inches across.

6 Brush two pizza pans or baking sheets with oil. Place the dough circles in the tins and push the edges up slightly to form a rim. Brush with oil.

7 Cover with the toppings and bake for 10–12 minutes, until golden.

BANANA NUT BREAD

Serve thick slices of this deliciously moist bread with mugs of steaming hot coffee for the perfect mid-morning snack.

INGREDIENTS

¹/₂ cup butter, at room temperature

¹/₂ cup sugar

2 eggs, at room temperature

1 cup white flour

1 teaspoon baking soda

¹/₄ teaspoon salt

1 teaspoon ground cinnamon

¹/₂ cup whole-wheat flour

3 large ripe bananas

1 teaspoon vanilla extract

¹/₂ cup chopped walnuts

MAKES 1 LOAF

1 Preheat the oven to 350°F. Carefully line the bottom and sides of a 9 x 5-inch pan with parchment paper and grease the paper.

2 With an electric mixer, cream the butter and sugar together until light and fluffy.

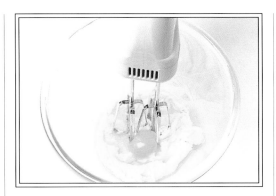

3 Add the eggs, one at a time, beating well after each addition.

4 Sift the white flour, baking soda, salt and cinnamon over the butter mixture and stir to blend. Stir in the whole-wheat flour.

5 With a fork, mash the bananas to a purée, then stir them into the mixture. Stir in the vanilla extract and walnuts.

6 Pour the mixture into the prepared pan and spread it evenly.

7 Bake for 50–60 minutes, until a skewer inserted in the center comes out clean. Let stand for 10 minutes before transferring to a wire rack to cool.

BLUEBERRY MUFFINS

These muffins are so delicious that they certainly won't be allowed to hang around on the serving plate for very long.

INGREDIENTS
1 cup flour
1 tablespoon baking powder
1/8 teaspoon salt
1/3 cup light brown sugar
1 egg
3/4 cup milk
3 tablespoons oil
2 teaspoons ground cinnamon
*1 cup fresh or thawed
frozen blueberries*

MAKES 8

VARIATION
Use other fruit instead of blueberries; blackcurrants, blackberries, cherries and raspberries all work just as well.

1 Preheat the oven to 375°. Grease a muffin tin.

2 With an electric mixer, beat all the ingredients except the blueberries together until smooth.

3 Using a wooden spoon, gently fold the blueberries into the creamed mixture.

4 Spoon the batter into the muffin tin, filling eight cups two-thirds full. Bake for about 25 minutes or until a skewer inserted in the center of a muffin comes out clean.

5 Let cool in the tin on a wire rack for 10 minutes, then unmold the muffins onto a wire rack and allow to cool.

HAZELNUT BROWNIES

 very chocoholic loves a brownie, and this recipe will prove no exception for them.

INGREDIENTS
2 ounces dark chocolate
5 tablespoons butter or margarine
1 cup sugar
7 tablespoons plain flour
1/2 teaspoon baking powder
2 eggs, beaten
1/2 teaspoon vanilla extract
1 cup skinned hazelnuts, roughly chopped

MAKES 9

1 Preheat the oven to 350°F. Grease an 8-inch square baking tin. In a bowl set over a pan of simmering water, or in a double boiler, melt the chocolate and butter. Remove from the heat.

2 Add the sugar, flour, baking powder, eggs, vanilla extract and half the hazelnuts to the melted mixture. Stir well with a wooden spoon.

3 Pour the batter into the prepared tin. Bake for 10 minutes, then sprinkle the reserved hazelnuts over the top. Return to the oven and continue baking for about 25 minutes, until firm to the touch.

4 Set the tin on a wire rack and let cool for 10 minutes, then unmold onto the rack and let cool completely. Cut the brownies into squares for serving.

CHOCOLATE CHIP AND MACADAMIA NUT COOKIES

plate of freshly baked cookies makes a welcome afternoon snack for everybody.

INGREDIENTS
1 cup flour
1 teaspoon baking powder
$^1/_4$ teaspoon salt
6 tablespoons butter or margarine
$^1/_2$ cup granulated sugar
$^1/_4$ cup light brown sugar
1 egg
1 teaspoon vanilla extract
$^3/_4$ cup chocolate chips
$^1/_2$ cup macadamia
nuts, chopped

MAKES 36

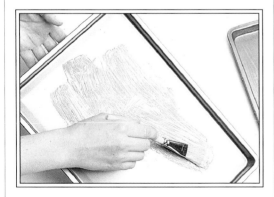

1 Preheat the oven to 350°F. Grease two or three baking sheets.

2 Sift the flour, baking powder and salt in a small bowl. Set aside.

3 With an electric mixer, cream the butter and sugars together. Beat in the egg and vanilla extract. Add the flour mixture and beat well with the mixer set on low speed.

4 Stir in the chocolate chips and half the macadamia nuts using a wooden spoon.

5 Drop the mixture by the teaspoonful onto the prepared baking sheets, to form $^3/_4$-inch mounds. Space the cookies generously as they will spread while baking.

6 Flatten each cookie lightly with a wet fork. Sprinkle the remaining macadamia nuts on the top and press them lightly into the surface.

7 Bake for 10–12 minutes, until golden brown. With a spatula, transfer the cookies to a wire rack to cool.

COOK'S TIP
Use any kind of chocolate chips you like for these cookies: white, milk, semisweet or a mixture.

PUMPKIN PIE

raditionally served at Thanksgiving, this pie is worth making at any time – whatever the celebration.

INGREDIENTS
2 cups cooked fresh or canned pumpkin
1 cup whipping cream
2 eggs
¹/₂ cup dark brown sugar
4 tablespoons light corn syrup
1¹/₂ teaspoons ground cinnamon
1 teaspoon ground ginger
¹/₄ teaspoon ground cloves
¹/₂ teaspoon salt

FOR THE PASTRY
3 cups flour
¹/₂ teaspoon salt
6 tablespoons cold butter, diced
*6 tablespoons cold white vegetable
shortening, diced*
3–4 tablespoons very cold water

SERVES 8

1 For the pastry, sift the flour and salt and rub in the fats until it resembles coarse bread crumbs. Stir in enough water to bind. Gather into a ball, wrap in plastic wrap and chill for 20 minutes.

2 Roll out the dough until it is ¹/₈-inch thick. Transfer to a 9-inch pie dish. Trim off the overhang. Roll out the trimmings and cut into leaf shapes. Moisten the edge of the pastry with a brush dipped in water.

3 Arrange the pastry leaves around the edge. Chill for 20 minutes. Meanwhile, preheat the oven to 400°F.

4 Prick the bottom of the pastry with a fork and line with crumpled parchment paper. Fill with dry beans and bake for 12 minutes. Remove the paper and beans and bake for 6–8 more minutes, until golden. Reduce the heat to 375°F.

5 Beat together the pumpkin, cream, eggs, sugar, corn syrup, spices and salt. Pour into the pastry shell and bake the pie for about 40 minutes, until set.

PECAN TART

Serve this scrumptious tart warm, accompanied by ice cream or whipped cream, if desired.

INGREDIENTS
3 eggs
1/8 teaspoon salt
scant 1 cup dark brown sugar
8 tablespoons dark corn syrup
2 tablespoons fresh lemon juice
6 tablespoons butter, melted
1 1/4 cups chopped pecans
1/2 cup pecan halves

FOR THE PASTRY
1 1/2 cups flour
1 tablespoon sugar
1 teaspoon baking powder
1/2 teaspoon salt
6 tablespoons cold unsalted butter, diced
1 egg yolk
3–4 tablespoons whipping cream

SERVES 8

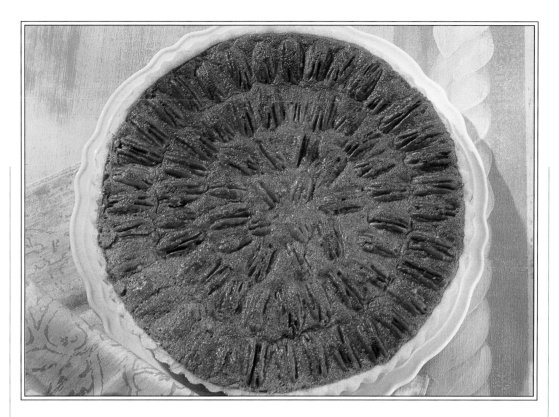

1 For the pastry, sift the flour, sugar, baking powder and salt into a mixing bowl. Add the butter and cut it in with a pastry blender until the mixture resembles coarse bread crumbs.

2 In another bowl, beat together the egg yolk and cream until blended.

3 Pour the cream mixture into the flour mixture and stir in with a fork.

4 Gently gather the pastry into a ball. On a lightly floured surface, roll out to 1/8 inch thick and transfer to a 9-inch pie dish. Trim off the overhang and flute the edge with your fingers. Chill for at least 30 minutes.

5 Preheat the oven to 400°F, with a baking sheet on the center shelf.

6 In a bowl, lightly whisk the eggs and salt. Add the sugar, corn syrup, lemon juice and butter. Mix well and then stir in the chopped pecans.

7 Pour the mixture into the pastry case and arrange the pecan halves in concentric circles on top.

8 Bake for 10 minutes. Reduce the heat to 325°F and continue baking for 25 more minutes. Allow to cool in the dish on a wire rack, and serve hot.

APPLE PIE

ou just can't beat a homemade apple pie, and this one is sure to be a regular feature on your table.

INGREDIENTS
2 pounds tart apples
1 tablespoon fresh lemon juice
1 teaspoon vanilla extract
1/2 cup sugar
1/2 teaspoon ground cinnamon
1 1/2 tablespoons butter or margarine
1 egg yolk
2 teaspoons light cream or half-and-half

FOR THE PASTRY
2 cups flour
1 teaspoon salt
1/2 cup vegetable shortening
4–5 tablespoons very cold water
1 teaspoon quick-cooking tapioca

SERVES 8

1 Preheat the oven to 450°F. For the pastry, sift the flour and salt into a bowl and rub in the shortening until the mixture resembles coarse bread crumbs.

2 Sprinkle in the water, 1 tablespoon at a time, tossing lightly with your fingertips or a fork until the dough forms a ball.

3 Divide the dough in half and shape each half into a ball. On a lightly floured surface, roll out one of the balls to a circle about 12 inches across.

4 Use the pastry to line a 9-inch tin, easing it in and being careful not to stretch it. Trim off the excess pastry and use the trimmings for decorating. Sprinkle the tapioca over the bottom of the pastry shell.

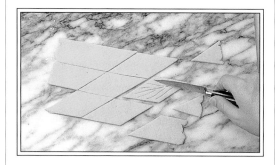

5 Roll out the remaining dough to a 1/8-inch thickness. Using a sharp knife, cut out eight large leaf shapes. Cut the trimmings into smaller leaf shapes. Score the leaves with the back of the knife to mark veins.

6 Peel , core and slice the apples into a bowl and toss with the lemon juice, vanilla extract, sugar and cinnamon. Fill the pastry shell with the apple mixture and dot with the butter.

7 Arrange the large pastry leaves in a decorative pattern on top of the apples. Decorate the edges with the smaller leaves.

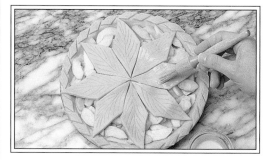

8 Combine the egg yolk and cream and brush over the leaves to glaze them.

9 Bake the pie for 10 minutes, then reduce the heat to 350°F and continue baking for 35–45 minutes, until the pastry is golden brown. Eat the pie hot, straight from the oven, or let the pie cool in the tin, set on a wire rack.

CHOCOLATE ICE CREAM

An easy-to-make dessert, this ice cream can be prepared a few days in advance and then brought out of the freezer when needed.

INGREDIENTS
2 cups whipping cream
3 egg yolks
1½ cups sweetened condensed milk
4 teaspoons vanilla extract
12 bourbon cookies, roughly crushed

MAKES 3 PINTS

1 Line a 2-pound loaf tin with foil, leaving enough overhang to cover the top.

2 In a mixing bowl, whip the cream until soft peaks form. Set aside.

3 In another mixing bowl, beat the egg yolks until thick and pale. Stir in the sweetened condensed milk and vanilla extract. Fold in the crushed cookies and whipped cream.

4 Pour the ice cream mixture into the prepared loaf tin. Cover it well with the foil overhang and freeze for about 6 hours, until firm.

5 To serve, remove the ice cream from the tin and peel off the foil. Cut into thin slices with a sharp knife.

CLASSIC CHEESECAKE

his baked cheesecake has a tangy lemon taste. Serve it with whipped cream for a divine dessert.

INGREDIENTS

$^3/_4$ *cup graham crackers, crushed*
4 cups cream cheese, at room temperature
1$^1/_4$ cups superfine sugar
grated rind of 1 lemon
3 tablespoons fresh lemon juice
1 teaspoon vanilla extract
4 eggs, at room temperature

SERVES 8

1 Preheat the oven to 325°F. Grease an 8-inch springform pan. Line it with a round of foil about 4 inches larger than the diameter of the pan. Press it up the sides to seal tightly.

2 Sprinkle the graham cracker crumbs in the base of the pan. Press to form an even layer.

3 Beat the cream cheese until smooth. Add the sugar, lemon rind and juice and vanilla and beat until blended. Add the eggs, one at a time, and beat just enough to blend.

4 Pour the cheesecake mixture into the prepared pan. Set the pan in a larger baking pan and pour enough hot water into the outer pan to come 1 inch up the sides of the cheesecake pan.

5 Bake for about 1½ hours, until the top of the cheesecake is golden brown. Let cool in the pan.

6 Run a knife around the edge to loosen, then remove the springform pan. Leave the cheesecake on the base and chill for at least 4 hours before serving.

DEVIL'S FOOD CAKE

 ot a cake for anyone counting calories, this chocolate delight is a real treat.

INGREDIENTS
4 ounces dark chocolate
1¼ cups milk
1 cup light brown sugar
1 egg yolk
2¼ cups self-rising flour
1 teaspoon baking soda
½ teaspoon salt
¾ cup butter or margarine,
at room temperature
1⅓ cups granulated sugar
3 eggs
1 teaspoon vanilla extract

FOR THE FROSTING
8 ounces plain dark chocolate
¾ cup sour cream
¼ teaspoon salt

SERVES 10

1 Preheat the oven to 350°F. Line two 8–9-inch round cake pans with parchment paper.

2 In a heatproof bowl set over a pan of barely simmering water, or in a double boiler, combine the chocolate and all but 1/4 tablespoons of the milk with the brown sugar and egg yolk. Cook, stirring, until smooth and thickened. Set aside to cool.

3 Meanwhile, sift the flour, baking soda, and salt into a small bowl and set aside.

4 With an electric mixer, cream the butter with the granulated sugar until light and fluffy. Beat in the whole eggs, one at a time. Mix in the vanilla extract.

5 On a low speed, beat the flour mixture into the butter mixture alternately with the remaining milk, beginning and ending with flour.

6 Pour in the cooled chocolate mixture and stir until just combined.

7 Divide the cake batter evenly between the two pans. Bake for 30–40 minutes, until a toothpick or skewer inserted in the center comes out clean.

8 Allow to cool in the pans on wire racks for 10 minutes, then unmold the cakes onto the wire racks and cool completely.

9 For the frosting, melt the chocolate in a heatproof bowl set over a pan of barely simmering water, or in the top of a double boiler. Remove the bowl from the heat and stir in the sour cream and salt. Allow to cool slightly.

10 Set one cake on a serving plate and spread it with a third of the chocolate icing. Place the second cake on top. Spread the remaining icing all over the top and sides of the cake, swirling it to make a decorative finish.

INDEX